Oceans of

Oceans of My Soul

Solo Sailing the South China Sea

Gillie Davies

Cover designed by Presence Advantage

This book is a work of fiction. Names, characters, places, and incidents either are products of the author's imagination or are used fictitiously. Any resemblance to actual persons, living or dead, events, or locales is entirely coincidental.

Gillie Davies
Visit my website at www.gilliesailssolo.com

Printed in the United Kingdom

First Printing March 2019

ISBN-9781795622608

Dedication

This is dedicated to my late father, who loved poetry and had the most wonderful speaking voice. He taught me the love of poetry.

Sometimes I can almost hear you

I can almost feel my hand in yours

as we walk across the fields towards the dawn

listening to the birds calling

hearing you recite poetry to me

I miss you daily and when I am quiet

I talk with you in my soul

Table of Contents

Forward

I have been writing poetry on and off since a child and although I have always struggled with spelling, the words often come in torrents in the middle of the night!

The proceeds of this book will help me to keep my little boat and hopefully continue my circumnavigation, that I first dreamt of over 30 years ago.

This is the first of a collection of poems that were written at a particularly trying time in my life, and, although to a large extent I had moved on from it, I was still in a vulnerable state of mind. As a Wednesday Child perhaps, I am full of woe as the saying goes, this collection has certainly come from sadness, loneliness and betrayal, but it was also inspired by the love and generosity I have been shown by friends and lovers and from sailing around the beautiful oceans and seas of our planet.

Thank you for purchasing this book in which, I am sure you will see, I share some of my passions.

Oceans of My Soul

If I were to drift
On an empty sea
Would I find peace there
Or
In the oceans of my soul

Courage

If I could take one ounce of the courage you believe I have

Could just swallow it and believe in me too

Move the stars with the gift of your love

I could take the moon and give it to you

If I could just know with the depth of your knowing

Be as strong as you see me to be

I could climb up to the top of this mountain

Take flight

Be free

Forgiving Myself

I forgive myself
For those weeks
When I momentarily thought
You were worth
More than me

Drifting

As a Dandelion seed

Drifting on the wind

Spinning on a breath

Barely visible in the sunlight

Landing imperceptibly lightly on the fertile soil

You were planted without my knowing

Deep into my blood stream

Pulsing through the veins of my life

Always there

Just a thought away

Scars and Wrinkles

The scars and wrinkles that you see
Are not from being perfect
They got here
Because I live my life
If you expect too much from me
You will be disappointed
Trust me
I always do my best
If you can't see that
You are the one who needs the specs

My Imagination

Stars on the ceiling of my room

A warm breeze blowing through my sails

Watch my dreams become real

Reaching up to where the pale moon lies

At peace with who I am and where I've been

I've seen it played a thousand times

Thought it was just my imagination

Yet here I am

Looking at the stars on the ceiling of my room

A Response to Loneliness

Personally

I think I've always been slightly insane

Being alone for me does not mean lonely

There is a sweet kind of freedom and yet

there are days when the wind is in my sails

I wish I could share

the beauty of the passage with a special one

Before

I had to compromise on when and to where I sailed

Now I can just lift my anchor and go!

It's funny how I often just stay

knowing that

Perfect Adventure

"I want the perfect adventure"
He said
"Oh! I'm so glad you do
in that case
Wake up every morning
Breathe in the new day
Live that day
For every moment of every day
Is the most perfect of all adventures "

Wonderful You

I want that core of steel
That I see running through you
Want to feel that strength
I see in your heart
To know that knowing
I hear in your wisdom
Your gentle bravery teaches me
It touches my soul
Gives me a new level to reach for
You are amazing to me
And, more wonderful still
I can call you friend

Not Now

By chance I turned and saw you
like a fleeting shadow in the sunlight
That was the moment
a millisecond of time
But I knew and I could see
All that stardust spilling from your pockets
almost a warning
almost a siren
I ignored them all
You were the one
and yet
I walk on without stopping
our time wasn't now
not in this life
I'll see you again
across some vast ocean
then we will dance until we fall into
dreams of each other

Boxes of You

I've packed you up in boxes ready to send away

It's funny how small a space you hold in them

Whilst in me you were taking up so much room

You were filling every corner of me

Every crack that appeared in my heart

So I've packed you up in boxes to send you away

Then I'll stick my broken bits back together

Add some stardust and some gold in the glue

And plant some flowers in the holes you left behind

If My Love

If my love
Breaks your wall
Into a thousand pieces
Open your soul
To new ideas
Then I am the miracle
You never saw coming

Love Was Here

Love was here
In the black
in the blue
in the yellow
Painful to touch now
Time will fade the colours
Inside the loss is still bruising my soul

The Sailor's Clock

Waking at the pre-dawn

I enjoy those quiet moments

Before even a bird stirs and flexes his vocal chords

I drink my coffee whilst the sun raises his head above the horizon

At night I start to relax as the sun sinks

As the coolness returns

before the stars come out to play

My best times are these

When I can reflect on the joys

When I am

In time with the tick

Of the sailor's clock

Sweet Memory

You crept in to this quiet place
I didn't know you were even there
Your breath was like a jasmine breeze
The sweet heady smell of love
It filled my nostrils and I could taste you
We found each other and danced
That slow, gyrating, sweet dance
The rhythm took us into distant places
It caught the beat of a far-away drum
We stretched, felt the moves
like we were water
we became the river, flowed in the love
reached the banks, kissing the shores
Then....like the night...you left......
The sun warms my body now....
you are just a memory

Hope of The Morning?

It's funny how
My best shots
Are at either end of my day
Is it hope of the morning?
Or joy in the evening?
Perhaps a little touch of longing

Askew

My world's a bit tilted
off centre
askew
I'm being and doing
yet nothing seems true
The season is turning
I'm here in a place
yet I feel like a misfit
don't belong in this space
I'll go through the motions
of living and breathing
but inside there are ghosts
of fear and of grieving
I'm changing
I feel it
from down in my soul
my autumn is coming
changing green into gold

Aging Badly

The tightness of my underwear
Has left marks upon my skin
And I wonder
For the umpteenth time
Why I ever let you in

In the fleshy folds of untamed fat
The rounded mounds of breasts
I can't believe
You ever found
attractiveness in this

The moisturising foundation cream
Has done little for the face
Where wrinkles round my mouth
Show the pain of wedded bliss
The weary shade of boredom
Are the lowlights in my hair
My eyes dance round the bedroom
Thanking god you are not there

I'm tired now of wishing
Dreaming things that never were
I am glad I am alone now
Not the abandoned half of pair
But Instagram and Facebook
Will show a different page
And I'm glad you cannot see
What has become of me with age

Softness to Strength

The softness of the nettle
Belies the sting of its leaf
As the willow bends
To the force of the wind
It looks to be submissive
The outer strength of the stone
Looks immovable and solid
Yet the gentleness of the water
Carves its patterns there
Perhaps the weakest has an inner strength
That the fighter has not known
The warrior may fall to the
Sting of the mosquito

Heavy Boots

Trudging in heavy boots
Muddy with all the care
Steel toe capped to stop the pain
Scuffed from almost going back
Trampling over all the lies
Stones in the tread
Clickety clacking on the floor of deceit
Kicking at the remains of our life

Dollars and Dreams

Oh Traveller

What journey are you on

Is it the one

You think will impress

To go where those before you

Took the same photographs

Is it to explore the hidden cultures

Of ancient peoples long since gone

And replaced by tourists

Weary men and women

Scratching a living from your foreign dollar and dream

Is it to find that hidden island
Where life is simple
Yet it has Wi-Fi and air-con
To give you the creature comforts
You cannot live without
And when you don't find it
That euphoria
That seemed so close to your grasp
What then my friend
Will your journey
Take an altogether different route

Letting Go

She stands at the soils edge
peers longingly towards the horizon
The water kisses her toes
as if it knows the time is fast approaching
She'll leave here soon
on the high tide
Pulled by a distant moon that drains her soul's blood
The petrels and terns
are dancing on the ocean's finger tips
and the osprey calls as he drifts
effortlessly on the thermals of her love
The stars are lighting the course she will sail
She'll leave nothing behind
but memories of gardens and trees
that lifted her high with hope and growth
until she saw her self
and finally loved her own image enough
to let go

Impact

Was it your intent to chill the warmth of this heart
To spread the dark cold stone like dry stone walls
Upturn equilibrium with self-doubt and regret
Or was it that you didn't take
Even a moment to consider your impact

Grief

Maybe it's grief over you
perhaps it's grief for me
tears seem to flow inwardly
relentlessly
as the water covers me
my breath is a little easier
concentration is the key
noticing when the dark thought comes

Guilty sorrows reaching hoping trying
falling deep within a dream
believing thoughts racing through the tunnels
Hearing unspoken
undetermined words
that never were mine to hear
Feeling strong arms
holding a body with love and tenderness
that were never mine to feel
Crying with fun and laughter
that were never mine to enjoy
emptiness like the last breath before drowning

I used to believe that if I pushed on
fought
strived and did all this
so fast
so hard
with avid determination
with all I could find within me
I would be in the right space
I used to believe that if I loved
with all my love
all my care
all my devotion
it would be enough..........
and it would have been
had I loved myself too
with equal ferocity

Perfect Choice

I chose you in that moment
you were perfect for it
We had many moments of perfect
interlaced with many that weren't
As those moments ticked by
The moments of perfect grew less and less
Until they were swallowed up
in the imperfect
and you were gone
Those perfect moments will leave
They will always leave
Because forever
my darling
is a myth

Forgetting You

Forgetting you
Feels like an open door in Winter
Until someone else
Lights the fire

All That Wild

Go outside
Feel the wind
Hear the night
Watch the stars
Think of me
I am all that wild
And more

Moments of Change

In moments of change
The pain and anguish
Of losing one's old skin
Is almost unbearable
Yet so absolutely necessary
To finally reveal the flawless self
One has been becoming for so long
And who's authenticity is
Beyond question

All Woman

I am fifty-eight years old

I haven't worn make-up in about 12 years

I'm wrinkled from being squished up

By all the love of my tribe

From the wind on my face

The freedoms of my life

And from the pain in my story

I wouldn't change a thing

Not with make-up or anything else

I am all woman

Anchored

Dock lines stowed and sails aloft

I finally left the was of us in the wake

Trimmed

Reached

reefed and full

I anchored in the now of me

Love Me

In the mornings when I wake

Watching the sun peep over the tops of the trees

I still believe

in those first rays of the dawn

I can't quite figure out why

Yet here I am again

Thinking solely of you

With your laugh and words as an ear worm

Constantly telling me that you really do

Love me

Delight

When you're quiet with yourself
Which words speak to you the loudest
Does music play in your ears
What builds the fiery passion in your soul?
Do the people and places of your life
Skip across the mind's eye in delight?

Gillie Davies

Keep on Walking

Open the door to the world
Step out from your comfort
Launch your heart to the breeze
Start walking
The fear is in your head
Look to the void of endless possibilities
You can keep on walking

Wild

My strength and power are in the knowing
That the love I give away
Is surplus to the love I still carry inside
That my soul spills from its purses
Coins of determination and fortitude
So that those in my wake
May feel the magnitude
Of the wild
Treacherous
warrior
Who is me

Inner Garden

I'm not here really
I'm in my inner garden
Working away
Pulling at weeds
Digging the soil
Making it fertile
I'm scouring the thistles
Zapping the creepy vines
That undermine the strength in my roots
Sometimes it's dark and cold here
But spring warmth and joyous rains will come
Then my garden may look different or
It may look as it always has
Maybe my garden is just the way it should be

Laughing Breezes

Stopping for a moment
Holding thoughts at bay
I hear the laughter of the breezes
Luring me to dream again
To hoist aloft the canvas
And sail out to far away

Walk with Me

Travel with me friend
Walking through the forests of doubt
Opening to the clarity of the glade
Travel with me

Travel gently friend
Tiptoeing through the fallen leaves
And broken hearts of lovers' past
Travel with me

Travel quietly friend
In the cacophony of wise words
Rustling through the grasses of truth
Travel with me

Travel boldly friend
When the howling storms of passion
Overwhelm the sodden earth
Travel with me

Travel consciously friend
Watching the lonely souls trudging
Yearning the companion of hope
Travel with me

Travel lovingly my friend
When the tears of loss overcome the pitiful
Wipe away the sorrows you carry and
Walk hand in hand with me.

Night Shift

On the night shift
The train drift
People moving in rhythm
Blindly trudging
On and on
Clickety clack clickety clack
Tic tocking their way through
Unseeing unbending
Stiff with resilience
Pushing pulling grabbing
holding easing loving hating
Grey dull tired
Sick and bloody tired

Eventually

You will fade
Eventually
They all do
When the seasons change
Step through the door
Fly north to summer

New Moon

Looking at the new moon alone
It's not what I had hoped for
I thought that I would be seeing it with you
Wrapped in your arms, feeling loved
I am here
Looking at the new moon alone

Looking at the new moon alone
I wish I could feel the joy
Of new chapters ahead to share
Wrapped in your arms feeling safe
I am still here
Looking at the new moon alone

Looking at the moon alone
Can you just take the step
To be here with me
To take me in your arms and be my one
I just don't want to be
Looking at the moon alone

Eclipse Catastrophe

A thud
Amongst the howling gale
Catapulting from my bunk
Catastrophe ensues
A brief panic
Engine fires
Gears engaged
Held fast as the tide falls
Yet smashed and smashed again
Countless times
Pleading with the gods I don't believe in
They do not hear me
They are not able
It is a futile state

Good Enough to Taste

It's raining and the sky has fallen
I'm waiting for you here
In the damp and dreary
I know you'll come
you promised me that
You'll stand dripping wet
mournful
Then
just as always
Your mouth edge will twitch
I'll watch the smile spread across your lips
Like icing running down the side of the cake
Sweet and enticing
good enough to taste

Make Your Day

Some people may try to spoil your day
Don't let them do that
Do let one beautiful person make your day
even if it is your beautiful self ♡

Goodbye

Today I finally said goodbye
Standing in my own earth
Holding my head above your wrath
No more the rescue remedy for your drama
I picked up the mat you wiped your feet on
Walked out and under my breath
said the final goodbye

Alone with Memories

Later when alone
With your memories
Will it become clear
That the real travelling
You did
Was not in the perfect photograph
Or the beautiful selfie
Not in the barefoot on beaches moments
Or the snow-capped mountains
The moments of your greatest trips
Were in the coldness of the lonely
And the detritus of humanity
For there in those seconds
You learned who you were

Sipping Nectar

Taken to a new horizon

Sit a while

Sip the nectar of morning

Feel the gossamer breeze touch your skin

Look out

observe

say nothing

Watch the wonder of clouds changing shape

Be the tenderness your heart desires

Drenched in Love

You, who would wound me
Have me stumbling in the dust
With tear streaks on smudged cheeks
You, who would cage me
Have me bound and shackled to your propriety
You, who to steal my joy
With sharpness of spite and meanness
Know that I am warrior
I am wild, free carrying my own burdens
Know, I will always rise from the oceans
Drenched in love

Aloneness

The Aloneness of the Solo Sailor
would be too much for many
however for me
the 3am rush of words that come
pushing through the writer's sleep
have no time for lonely

Birthmark

I wanted to be the dried ink on your page
The indelible
I wanted to be the blemish on your skin
The birthmark
I wanted to be the moon in your night sky
The glint on dew
I wanted to be the stars behind your storm clouds
The glimmer of hope
You were all of these for me

Quiet Moments

Let us sit on the rocks you and I
at sunset
Listening to the waves lapping
the final birdsong
I want to hear your breathing
in quiet moments
Then
later when we are drenched in our love
When our desires and dreams
have been laid naked
As I trace my fingers over your chest
I will climb into your soul and sleep
Safe in the arms of our bliss

Cobweb Kisses

The breeze
like cobweb kisses
Brushed away my sorrow
Took me to a new bay
Where I anchor
Write my new story
Of my bravery
My courage

Be You

"They" are not you

don't wear your shoes

don't walk your path

are not minding your own business

don't need to be heard by you

are not on your journey

You are not "they"

Be you

The Lonely

They all end up here
Eventually
The wild things
The lonely
Misfits explorers
Lovers of whispers
Of slow rhythmic dances
To move in the rolling and drifting
The endless searching
For the eutrophic lake
And dive in breathless with desire
Stretching in feline delight
Wanton and raw
Sucking in the pleasure and ecstasy
Never quite getting enough of her generosity

Extraordinary You

Under this sky I know you

Under that sky you have lived

Under this sky I believed in you

Under that sky I saw the real you

You are beautiful

You are amazing

Under any sky you are extraordinary

Change

Under the new moon
He makes the change
He's walking away
Can't stand the pain
The cold rain drenching through to his skin
A north wind blowing her perfume away
He knows he'll never hold her again

For the Love Of You

In small moments
those between asleep and awake
There I miss you to my very core
The chasm it leaves almost sucks me into oblivion
It's here, in those brief seconds that I reach
here as my fingers touch the empty pillow
Here my heart breaks for the love of you

Wildest Dreams

I am the

...Salt spray from the breaking wave

...Wildest dream you dare to remember

...Torch to light the flame

...Wind that blows away inhibition

...One just out of reach

...Secret just around the bend of the track

...Lover who takes you beyond bliss

...Only place you want to be

...End and your beginning

Washed Together

Side by side continents apart
I am with you, holding your hand
You holding mine
We watch and listen to the sounds
All is quiet
just your breathing and mine
Two places yet one
I hear your heart beating
And reaching over you take mine
So I am watching
feeling your hands caressing
Exploring those small places where I am
Then stretching I take yours
Beating rhythmically with mine.
We, in tune, same tones
trebles and basses calling each other
Clouds are gathering
Feel the rain dripping in tune with us
We are washed together now as one

Emerging

There are no answers to the questions
Yet still they're in my head
Picking at the scabs left from your treachery
Beating me bloody
When I'm low enough
Kicking me silently as I lie in my sadness
The world won't catch me crying
You'll be the last to know how this pain hurts
I will not drown here in my fear and my longing
I'll take a deep breath
Sit cross legged
Beneath the surface of anxiety
Watching
Reflecting
Allowing myself to emerge

Black Bee

The black bee didn't come today
He doesn't know it's today
The swallows clicked and swooped
Fish chattered at the waterline
A dragonfly smaller than a seamstress' pin
Perches on the mizzen stay wire
Sea eagles call
The sun rises
None of them know me
Black bee doesn't know I notice his absence
Swallows don't tick and swoop for me
Dragonfly and tiny gecko just are
Monkeys are busy with their own business
And the moon sets

Reaching Bliss

Is it here
The place where my soul can speak
a moment where my heart can rest
from all the cares and troubles I carry
Are you here
To hold me like it's the last chance
trace your fingers over my mouth
then to kiss me that beautiful kiss
Is it now
When all the storms have passed
that moment so bright with love
when my bliss reaches its peak

You'll Find Me

Where the garden meets the sea
That my love is where I'll be
Where the sea breezes whistle through branches
Where you hear the crashing of the ocean
In this place
I am the wind caressing your cheeks
I am the wing tips of the Osprey
Diving for her fish

The Invitation

To do at least part of this alone

Having lived this life alone mostly

Even with people around

I've been lucky

Have loved like life depended upon it

Lived like tomorrow isn't coming

Sailed an ocean

May sail another

You touched me today

Like I didn't know anyone could

How did that happen

Your beauty is breath taking

Your wild is thrilling

I want to sail your ocean

Come sail mine

Between the Blue

Now between the red and blue
Under the last remnants of moon
The first dusting of sun
Catching the essence of the world
Before the bustle and hustle
Before the spoken words
Whilst it's still a peaceful place
This is the moment to be

I Wonder

Some days I struggle to keep the tears at bay
They are welling up and my eyes
Are not only watery with age
I wonder how you feel
I wonder if your tears are close too
Which is the craziest thing
Because you are a hustler
Who plays with women's emotions
Just like mine
I wonder why you were sent to me
Because everything happens for me
Why do these feelings of sadness come
Why do I need them I wonder

Northern Coasts

It's the soul of you I crave

Your essence

Your creases

Your dark blood

Running in those secret places

Your soil

your fertile mind

It's your scared woman I hold

Your bold heart

your challenge

Your strength in wanderlust

A smile you bring at

Just knowing you're there

in cold Northern coasts

Exquisite Reality

She is pricelessly exquisite
In her beautiful reality

Walk Gently

Walk gently down these paths
As you're conjuring your magic
Footprints of others lie before you
That have flattened love
And left broken bits of me

Are you the book I can read forever
Can I live in your vellum
Lie in the arms of words on a page
Smell your ink as it traces across my skin
Walk gently darling
Walk gently

Walk gently along my shores
Please don't crush the sea shells you find
Collect them
Keep them safe
They are my dreams
Some may have little chinks
They are still valid
Still worth keeping

Are you the whale song
To serenade me for a hundred years
Where I dive into the music of your heart
Swim amongst your desires
Feel your blood caressing my soul
Walk gently darling
Walk gently

Acknowledgements

Thank you to all those who have encouraged me to publish this first book. In particular, I would like to say an extra special thank you to: -

Frances Garner: Fellow sailor, poet and dear friend, who kept on telling me to write and publish these verses. Who has supported me throughout the entire process, spent hours on reading, grading and arranging, texting, telephoning and most of all, did it with love.

Helen Davies: Best friend, for checking and rechecking spellings and punctuation, encouragement, love and friendship over the years.

Dennison Berwick: Author and fellow sailor, for pointing me in the right direction to get published, for lunches and discussions over content and printing options.

Stuart Mossop: Fellow Sailor and friend, for reading and re-reading drafts, critiquing, encouraging and keeping me smiling.

Muz Mason: Friend, for reading and constructively commenting on the first drafts and ideas.

Angela Davies: My mother, for encouraging me to sail solo, weekly phone calls and without whom, I would have struggled to keep afloat.

Presence Advantage: Friend and artist, for producing such an amazing cover from my original photograph of Tuppenny.

Printed in Great Britain
by Amazon